# PATTERNS OF CHRISTIAN COMMUNITY

# Patterns of Christian Community

*A Statement of Community Order*

Edited by Stephen B. Clark

SERVANT BOOKS
Ann Arbor, Michigan

Book design by John B. Leidy

Available from Servant Publications, Box 8617
Ann Arbor, Michigan 48107

ISBN 0-89283-186-3
Printed in the United States of America

1 2 3 4 5 6 7 8 9 10 89 88 87 86 85 84

# *Contents*

# Introduction

*Patterns of Christian Community* has been written from the experience of a body of Christians who have sought to live together the Lord's call to love one another. It is therefore based on the teaching in scripture of what it means to be brothers and sisters in the Lord, read in the light of efforts of dedicated Christians through the centuries to be faithful not only to the Lord but also to one another. Behind the variety of structures and forms that Christians have used, there is a remarkable similarity in the basic approach to order—at least among Christians who recognize that being a Christian involves a personal commitment to other Christians because of the Lord.

*Patterns of Christian Community* is the product of experience. The truths in it have been lived, and the statement of them has developed as a result of practice. Many of these truths are here because of experiencing the bad consequences of omitting them. The statement in its present form has been written to make that experience useful to a wide group of Christians. In our time, many Christians have sought to live out Christian community and have failed because they have not known about or have not accepted some of the truths in this statement.

This statement is written for certain groups, groups that could be called "communities," because they have a corporate life, because they have an ordered and disciplined life and are therefore more than just informal groupings, and because the members have a brotherly commitment to one another and not just organizational commitments to the body. In using the word "community" this way, the statement makes use of a word (*koinonia*) that is employed in the New Testament to refer to the sharing of Christians in the same spiritual and material goods, but it uses the word in a slightly different (and nowadays more common) sense to refer to the groups themselves who share their lives and goods together.

This statement is written primarily for groups of people who live in their own homes and work in normal secular jobs, but who wish to relate to one another in a committed way as brothers and sisters in the Lord. It is also written for what might be called "communes" or "religious communities," that is, groups of people who live in the same building or on the same plot of ground and administer all their finances together. Both types of Christian groups can make use of the statement because most of the truths are common to both and the differences between them are taken into account. The statement, however, could also be used more broadly by other groupings of Christians (fellowships, parishes, congregations, religious organizations) who are looking for a fuller sharing and life together, since it presents many principles that apply to them as well, although they have to be careful to discern what applies to their situation.

*Patterns of Christian Community* addresses an important topic that arises in the life of "full" communities: pastoral care that involves a certain kind of authority over the lives of the members—what is called "government" in the statement.

There have been numerous examples of groups of Christians that have attempted to have full community life either without adequate government or without regard to the scriptural safeguards on government in community. Consequently, there have been instances of abuses of authority in Christian groups as there have been, even more notably, in non-Christian and semi-Christian cults. The statement attempts to present the biblical norms which should control and shape government in Christian community.

Similarly, there is an emphasis in the statement on resolving disputes and dealing with wrongdoing according to scriptural principles. These also offer helpful and corrective wisdom for dealing with common problems that arise among Christians, including the handling of situations where there may have been wrongdoing by leaders.

This statement envisions many types of local groupings, including those who regard themselves as local churches and those who do not claim the fullness of church life or authority, those who are parishes or congregations or cells of a larger grouping and those who are independent of such ties. It is written to be of service to a very wide group of Christians, including Orthodox, Catholics and Protestants and including likewise ecumenical (interchurch or interdenominational) bodies that seek to relate to one another with a brotherly commitment. Therefore, it avoids many subjects that would normally be considered part of church order and seeks to avoid many matters that are disputed among Christians. It is, in short, incomplete and needs to be supplemented.

This statement is written with local communities in mind that belong to larger groupings as well as ones that do not. It does not, however, treat the question of how local communities should relate to one another, or to larger groupings. Its primary application is to local bodies, but it can also be applied to regional, national or international groupings that give governing authority to a corporate body with a president, if they have a communal commitment to one another. If the statement is used for such groups, it needs to be supplemented with decisions about how the local communities relate to one another and to the larger community.

*Patterns of Christian Community* has come out of a corporate process. It is the result of many discussions and decisions over more than a decade. We have adopted it to be our pledge of good government, a pledge that we can be held accountable to. We expect it to be a protection against arbitrary government as well as a spur to faithfulness to Christian principles of righteousness in the exercise of authority. May more and more Christian leaders see the value of good government and be willing to give the necesssary time to the study of the Lord's teaching about it.

# Preface

OUR LORD JESUS on the night he died said that the
mark of his disciples would be the love that they
had for one another. He concluded his last supper Jn 3:34[a].
by praying for those who would come to believe in
him that they would be completely one, even as he
and the Father are one. We have committed Jn 17:20-21
ourselves as a body to love one another and to live
the unity that the Lord Jesus obtained for us at the
price of his blood. To preserve that love and unity, Col 1:20
we have to understand the community relation-
ship that we are in, and we have to respect and
support the order that makes a corporate life
together possible. As the apostle Paul said after
laying down some directions on order among
Christians, "God is not a God of confusion, but of
peace." That peace, and the good order that 1 Cor 14:33
expresses it and serves it, is the bond that preserves the unity of the Spirit. We therefore wish to Eph 4:3
set down the main outlines of the order of a
Christian community so that community members might commit themselves more firmly to
their life together, so that those responsible for the
direction of communities might serve their brothers and sisters with greater wisdom and authority,
and so that others may understand better the life
we are trying to live.

This statement concerns only our corporate life as Christians who seek to love one another in the Lord. It does not touch upon much of Christian doctrine or moral teaching. It does not include much of what a Christian needs to know to love his brothers and sisters in the Lord. It is simply a statement of community order. But as such it treats matters which are lifegiving and a source of power for the Christian people.

## Notes

a. Scripture passages are normally placed in the margin parallel to the end of the sentence they pertain to. Sometimes they are placed at the beginning of paragraphs or, rarely, subsections of paragraphs, and in that case they pertain to the whole paragraph.

The scripture references are not complete for most topics. They are a selection of the passages which provide the foundation for the statement.

# *I. Basic Commitment*

## *1. Our relationship as a body*[a]

We believe that the Lord Jesus Christ has called us to be a people, a body, a community, brothers and sisters in him. He has called us together and united us so that we might serve him and glorify him as a body, and so that we might love one another as brothers and sisters and encourage one another to love and serve the Lord above all. He has entrusted us with a mission, and he will lead us by his Spirit to know that mission and be faithful to it.

Our relationship as a body rests first of all upon what the Lord Jesus has done to make us one. He has reconciled us with God by the blood of his cross, and in making us one with his Father, he has Col 1:20
brought us into a relationship with one another,
making us brothers and sisters in one body. We are Eph 2:15-16
one body because Christ has made us one, and because we accepted that oneness from him as his gift when we received our redemption.

Our relationship as a body also rests upon our commitment together.[b] We have solemnly committed ourselves to the Lord and to one another to
be a body, to love and serve the Lord together. We 2 Chr 15:12, 23:16
have committed ourselves to the mission the Lord entrusts to us, to all those things which make our life together possible, and to one another as our brothers and sisters. Our commitment is no longer

a matter of our own individual decision, but we
1 Tm 6:12 have bound ourselves before many witnesses to
the Lord and one another—out of love for the
Lord and one another. We wish to fulfill that
commitment with the same steadfast love and
faithfulness that the Lord shows in his commitment to us.

## *2. The nature of our commitment*

We are committing ourselves to the Lord as his
people and to one another as brothers and sisters.
Our commitment is a full commitment, a com-
1 Pt 1:22 mitment that involves our whole lives. We are not
simply committing ourselves to certain activities
or obligations, but we are committing ourselves to
a relationship which reaches to everything in our
lives. We may not do everything together or
administer our finances jointly or live in one place,
Acts: 4:32; 1 Jn 2:3 but we do put our lives in common and make them
available for the mission our body has from the
Lord for the service of our brothers and sisters.

Our commitment is first of all to love and serve
Mt 22:37 God himself. We wish to love him fervently and
serve him with full dedication. We wish to obey
him unreservedly and to do all that we do with full
faith in him. We desire to give our whole lives to
him, to follow his Son Jesus, and to live more fully
in the Holy Spirit. We come together to pledge our
lives to him. We agree to seek the Lord with all our
2 Chr 15:12; 23:16 heart and with all our soul and to be his people.

We commit ourselves, as well, to one another. As we pledge ourselves to love and serve the Lord and to be his people, we receive one another as brothers and sisters, members of the same body.

We gladly commit ourselves to love each other in
purity of heart, fervently. We commit ourselves to 1 Pt 1:22
be one another's servants and to lay down our lives 1 Jn 3:1;
for one another. We recognize that because we are Phil 2:3-8
one body in Christ and have put our lives in
common, that we are no longer masters and
owners of our own lives, but our lives belong to Rom 12:5;
one another. We are ready to meet one another's 1 Cor 12:25-26
needs by our personal help and resources. We will Rom 12:13; 1 Jn 3:17
look upon one another's welfare as our own. Mt 22:39

We commit ourselves, further, to be a people
that the Lord can use as a body. We therefore
commit ourselves to be one in heart and soul, in
full accord and of one mind. We will put that Acts 4:32; Phil 2:2
oneness above our personal concerns, and we will Phil 2:4
pursue peace within the body, guarding our unity
against every threat. We commit ourselves to Eph 4:3
support those things that make life in one body
possible. We will be present at the gatherings of
the community. We will respect and support the Heb 10:25
pattern and order of our life together. We will Col 2:5
support the community and its mission with our
personal lives and resources and be ready to
sacrifice to the degree that is necessary for the
community to fulfill the call of the Lord to us as a
body. Phil 4:14-16

Finally, we commit ourselves to live our lives in
true righteousness and holiness. All of our lives Eph 4:24
must be worthy of the calling to which we have
been called. None of our lives is lived by ourselves Eph 4:1
alone, but all of our lives belong to the Lord and to
our brothers and sisters. Therefore our faithful- Acts 4:32
ness to our commitment to live personal lives of
righteousness and holiness is a concern of the
whole body, and we are willing to give an account

1 Jn 1:7; Jn 3:21 of the way we live our lives to our brothers and
Eph 5:8 sisters. We wish to walk as children of the light.

We recognize that when our lives are in community with those of our brothers and sisters, our lives are under the order of the community as a whole. In everything we do, we are members of a body and not just isolated individuals. Therefore decisions about our lives are decisions which are the concern of the whole body, and we are ready to make them according to the order of the community with the good of the whole body and of our brothers and sisters in mind. At the same time we can expect the support of our brothers and sisters in everything that we do, and not just in those things that we do together as a community. We are committed to support one another in all the commitments, such as family and occupational commitments, that may involve people outside of our community. We have put the entirety of our lives in common, therefore we can have the support of the body in everything we do, and we serve as members of the body wherever we are.

We recognize also that the commitment we have to one another is both the same that all Christians have and is particular to our body. Our commitment is to love one another as brothers and sisters in Christ the way any group of Christians would. Yet at the same time, we do belong to a particular body of Christians, a body which has a particular call and mission from the Lord. Our commitment might lead us in different ways from other Christians, because it is a commitment to a particular body that not all Christians belong to. We do wish to serve the Lord in this body, love these our brothers and sisters, and follow the Lord in whatever call and mission he has for the body.

## *3. Our relationship to others*

Our desire is to relate to all Christians as our brothers and sisters in the Lord, because they are our brothers and sisters in the Lord. Yet we recognize that we cannot fully relate to them that way until they are ready to enter into such a relationship with us and be faithful to it. We therefore pledge ourselves to work for a full unity among Christians, and we commit ourselves to relate in as brotherly a way as possible to all who believe in the Lord.

Our desire is to relate to the whole human race as our brothers and sisters in the Lord, because God loves them all and wants to unite them all to himself in his Son. In order for them to become our brothers and sisters in the Lord, however, they must turn to Christ and be joined to him. We therefore pledge ourselves to share the good news of the Lord Jesus Christ with all those we can, and Mt 28:18-20; Col 4:5
we commit ourselves to relate in as loving a way as Mt 5:43-48; Gal 6:10
possible to everyone until God be all in all. Eph 1:23

# Notes

a. The commitment described here is either the commitment to a local community or the commitment to a broader community, or both. It is here to be understood primarily as the commitment to a local body of Christians, but that same commitment can apply to Christians in other localities if they form a body together.

b. Some Christians see baptism as a sufficient commitment to one another. Others would add a profession of faith as established by a church or denomination. Others would add explicit covenants, either following the pattern described in II Chronicles to renew or make explicit the already existing covenant established by the Lord, or to add a further commitment as a body that is not simply contained in the basic Christian commitment. The statement allows for all of these, but we must recognize that a corporate commitment will not be as effective as it could be unless people are brought to state their acceptance of an explicit commitment to one another and unless that commitment is either made or reaffirmed as an adult.

# II. Functioning as a Body

## 1. Life, Mission and Service

The Lord calls a community of Christians to
love God, to love one another, and to love all men. Mt 22:37-9; Gal 6:10
He also entrusts to them a mission: to make known
the way of salvation and to receive people into the
community, providing a new way of life for them. 1 Pt 2:9; Phil 1:27
In addition, he might entrust to a community of
Christians a mission that is particular to them.
Therefore the members of the community must
dedicate themselves to service in order to maintain
the life of the community and to make its mission
successful. They must be men and women who Rom 12:11
give their lives for others, and who are no longer
their own. They must be men and women who Jn 13:13; 1 Jn 3:16;
make the gifts the Lord has given them freely 1 Pt 4:8
available to the needs of the community. Only a 1 Pt 4:10-11
community of servants of God can be a body,
carrying out the mission the Lord has given them.

## 2. Building up the body

Both Christian communities and individual
Christians must be built up and strengthened in
the Lord in order to fulfill the Lord's purpose for
them. When the Lord calls people to serve within
the community, he calls them to build up the
body: to both strengthen the brothers and sisters
individually, and the body as a whole. Moreover, 1 Cor 3:5-9

the responsibility to build up the body is not entrusted exclusively to a special group within the community. All the members of the community are responsible to work actively to build one another up in the Lord, and to build up the community as a whole. A community of Christians is a body that builds itself up in love as each part works properly.

1 Thes 5:11; Col 3:16; Eph 4:7-15
Eph 4:16

The most important position held by any member in the community is the same: that of son or daughter of God and brother or sister in the Lord. The most important community service performed by any member of the body is the same: that of loving one another. Love for one another should be carried on daily both in community activities and in informal meeting. There are special jobs within the community and special positions of service, but those jobs and positions, if they are functioning well, should support the ongoing work of building one another up which is done by all the members of the community in their daily lives. In turn, this mutual building up enables community members to live as the Lord teaches them, and to carry out the mission which he entrusts to them.

### *3. Serving as a body*

Rom 12:3-8; 1 Cor 12:12-26

The Lord intends Christians to live and serve him not merely as individuals, but as part of a body. He therefore calls them to an interdependence upon one another. Each member does his part of the needed service, and must rely upon others to do the rest. All the members must serve together in the kind of order which allows them to function in a united way as one body.

The different services that members of a Christian community perform often arise out of the relationships and groupings in which they take part. Most community members belong to families, and within those families they are husbands or wives, parents or children. Most community members belong to smaller groupings within the community, formed for the sake of support or service, and they hold various responsibilities within those groupings. Many community members have an occupation, and consequently engage not only in work, but in relationships with employers, employees, and co-workers. As a result of all these groupings and relationships, each member of the community will find himself or herself in a position of service that will differ from that of others in the community.

Eph 5:21-6:9; Col 3:18-4:1; 1 Pt 2:13-3:7; Lk 3:10-14

The different services that members of a Christian community perform also arise out of different gifts that the Lord has given them. The Holy Spirit equips individual Christians for service in different ways. Some can prophesy powerfully. Others have charisms of healing. Others have more facility to speak with spiritual wisdom. Some gifts stand out more strikingly, because the power of God manifests itself in a more obvious supernatural way through them, or because the person uses the gift in a public way. Other gifts are more hidden, and may lead members of the body to services which primarily support others, or to services which are carried out in daily living situations such as home or office. Because of the differences in the equipment the Lord has provided for service, members of the community will find themselves performing services that will differ from those of others in the community.

1 Cor 12:4-11; Rom 12:3-8; 1 Pt 4:10-11

Acts 14:23; 1 Tm 3:1-7; Ti 1:5-9

Within a Christian community, the Lord has established certain positions for its unity and good order. The overall governmental responsibility belongs to elders, who care for the whole community and who watch over the service of its members, in order that everyone's service might contribute to the united functioning of one body. Others work under the elders to care for smaller groupings within the community or to support the elders in their work; hence, they make the governmental care and order more effective throughout the body. The Lord also gives some members the gifts to be prophets, teachers, and evangelists. As these gifts become mature and tested, members with these gifts take on a significant responsibility for building up the body as a whole, and many of them serve as elders.

1 Cor 12:28; Acts 13:1

## *4. Authority in the body*

Mt 18:18-20

Within a Christian body, there are many types of authority. Everyone who belongs to the body exercises spiritual authority as a son or daughter of God and as a brother or sister in the Lord. With that authority comes a responsibility for the welfare and mission of the community, as well as power from God to serve. Everyone in the community has some moral authority arising from his knowledge or capability or resources or gift from God, and that moral authority properly used should provide influence in community life and service. Certain members of the community, because of the positions they hold, have the governmental authority to decide about or to direct the life and service of the community. Among these, the elders, under the presiding elder, have the highest authority within the community, because to them has been entrusted the overall responsibility for the community. Under them, some hold authority because it has been delegated to them by the elders. Others hold an authority that has been delegated to them directly by God, either because of a natural relationship (as the fathers of families), or because of a special call from God (as do the prophets). Within the community, however, all authority must be exercised subject to the authority of the body of elders, who are answerable to the Lord for the unity, welfare, and faithfulness of the body.

There are many protections against the improper exercise of authority in a Christian community, and they should be used; but there is no final guarantee other than faithfulness to the Lord. Following good order brings peace and unity to the body, and it provides protection in the exercise of authority, but it by no means guarantees that everything will be done correctly. Those who exercise authority in the body must submit themselves to the Lord, to his revealed word, and to his present direction. They must serve him in righteousness and learn his wisdom about how to fulfill their responsibilities. As they do these things, they can add to the authority that comes from proper authorization the certainty that comes from speaking and acting in God's word.

## *5. The Lord builds his body*

The Lord wants to build his people. He speaks to them, he teaches them, strengthens them, and helps them. He works by the direct action of the Holy Spirit in them. He works by intervening in the circumstances of their lives. He also works

Eph 3:14-20; Phil 1:6, 2:13

Jn 14:15-17, 23, 25-26, 16:12-15

through the mutual service of members of the
Heb 12:5-11; body. There are many things which he will do only
Jas 1:2-4 through a brother or sister.

1 Cor 12:14-31;
Rom 12:3-8;
1 Pt 4:10-11

His desire is to direct and form his people, but his ability to do so is often limited by those through whom he has chosen to do his work. Each body of Christians and each individual Christian must therefore turn to the Lord in faith and obedience, and follow him faithfully. As they do, he will build up and work through his body.

# III. Elders

## 1. The position of elder

Good order is established in a Christian community through the work of those who have been given positions of responsibility and the authority to govern others. While laws and procedures and methods may be a great help in the common life of Christians, even more important is the service of those who are the governors of each grouping of Christians. Jesus Christ wishes to work through his servants, to whom he has given authority so that they might order and build up his people. Eph 4:8-14

In a Christian community, elders are appointed Acts 14:23
to be the governors of the community as a whole.
They are called elders, because they are men who
are mature in experience as dedicated Christians
and normally in age, and who are the kinds of men
who are respected by others and followed easily. Nm 11:16-17
They preside over the community, leading the
whole body at gatherings of the community and in
the ongoing life of the community. They govern, 1 Thes 5:12
shaping and directing the body as a whole and the
groupings and individuals in the body. They Heb 13:17
watch over everything and everyone to see that
everything goes well and that the body is built up. Acts 20:28
They are shepherds, ruling over, caring for and
feeding all the community. They represent the 1 Pt 5:2
community, being the ones who can speak and act

on behalf of the body as a whole within the community and being the ones who can relate for the community to those outside the community. They have the final authority in the community for the order and direction of the life of the body, and nothing can be said to be an action of the community without their approval.

## *2. The elders as a body*

The elders as a body are the highest authority in the community. There will be areas of responsibility entrusted to the individual elders. There will be authority and order within the body of elders itself. But the elders as a body are the highest authority in the community. No individual elder is free to serve as a governor in any area or over any people without the agreement of the body of elders or of the presiding elder. It is a great protection for the community and for the individual elders to have the government of the community in a body of good elders.

1 Tm 5:22; Ti 1:5; Acts 12:17, 15:19

There will be a presiding elder chosen to be over the body of elders. He will speak for the body of elders, and the elders cannot act as a body except under his presidency or the presidency of someone he appoints. He will govern the elders as a body and individually with a responsibility to correct them and direct them in their work. As the number of elders increases, his responsibility for the personal lives and service of some of the other elders can be entrusted to others of the mature elders, but he will still keep final responsibility for them all. He will preside over the direction of the community, but he will not be free to make major decisions on his own without the approval of the whole body of elders or without the counsel of the other elders given openly in the gatherings of the elders. He will be responsible for overseeing the process of appeal from an elder's decision within the community. His own service will be subject to the review of the whole body of elders, and some of the more mature elders will care for him in his personal life and service.

If the elders are going to be more than just a body in name, they must love one another and be committed to one another personally. They should not be a group of functionaries or officeholders, but they should be brothers who serve and care for one another and who protect one another from the work of Satan. They should be open with one another, free to speak their mind to one another, free to call upon one another in need. They should guard their unity with great earnestness, resolving all difficulties and disputes—both those within the group and those between individual elders—as rapidly as possible. They should be submissive to the presiding elder and support him in his work of leading them. If the elders do not love one another and are not one, the other brothers and sisters will not love one another and be one.

Jn 13:34-35

## *3. Elders directing the community*

As the governors of the community, the elders under the presiding elder have the responsibility for directing the community. They can and should entrust areas of responsibility with authority to set direction to individuals and groups within the community. They can and should listen to the opinions of the whole community or at least of the more mature and responsible members of the community about the direction of the community. But the final responsibility for direction belongs to the body of elders, and they should not give over responsibility for decisions concerning the order of the community, for the major directional decisions in the community, for any decisions binding on all the members of the community, or for the main outlines of the teaching of the community to any other person or group within the community. They should protect the community from teachings or trends that are unsound or do not further the life and mission of the body.

Acts 20:29-31; 1 Tm 1: 3-5, 6:20; 2 Tm 1:14, 4:1-5; Ti 1:9

The elders are, to be sure, subject in their decision-making to the scriptures,[c.] to the constitution of the community,[d.] to any true message from the Lord, and to any person or body that is over the community. But it is their responsibility to preside over the body in its efforts to understand scriptures, to interpret what is in accord with the constitution of the community and what would constitute a change in the constitution, to test all messages that purport to be from the Lord, and to relate on behalf of the community to any person or body that is over the community.

If the elders are to fulfill their responsibility to direct the community, they must be men who are dedicated to do whatever the Lord wants and everything the Lord wants. They must be men of prayer who seek the Lord together. They should study the word of God together and be responsive to the Spirit of God together. They should avoid being polemical, critical, contentious or rigid in their discussions, but they should be respectful, teachable, kind, pursuing peace and oneness of mind and heart. Yet nonetheless, they should

Acts 1:14, 13:2

Acts 11:15-19, 13:1-4, 15:28, 16:10

Jas 3:13-18; 2 Tm 2:23-26

preserve a strong commitment to the truth and a dedication together to guard what has been entrusted to them, preserving the true teaching of Christ. 1 Tm 6:20

## *4. Elders watching over the community*

As those who watch over the community, the elders are responsible to see that everything is going well in the community. They should see that everything that happens in the community builds up the body and furthers the mission entrusted by the Lord to the body. They should encourage what is good and correct what is wrong. They should exercise real supervision over every activity of the body. No service can be considered a service of the community without their approval and ongoing supervision. They should take an active concern for the good of the community and its mission. If there is a problem in the life of the community, they should resolve it or see that it is resolved. If the service of the Lord is failing in any way, they should move it forward with zeal. They will have to present their work to the Lord to be tested, so that what passes the test can stand to the glory of God. 1 Cor 3:10-15

## *5. Elders caring for community members*

As the shepherds of the community, the elders are responsible for those who belong to the community. The welfare of the members of the community, both their spiritual and their material welfare, is entrusted to them. They should see that the widows and orphans, the poor, the sick, the weak, the guests and any needy are cared for

adequately. They should not neglect to admonish
the disorderly, the negligent, and those who are
1 Thes 5:14 going astray. They should preserve discipline in
the community, knowing that they will have to
Heb 13:17 give an account. They should watch over the
strong and committed, seeing that they receive
what they need to grow and to serve effectively.
They should give special attention and training to
those who can care for others, so that the needs of
2 Tm 2:2 all can be met. They should unfailingly represent
the needs of the whole body and of its mission to
the individuals in the community as those individuals make personal decisions. They should
settle any disputes between members of the
community that the members cannot settle them-
Mt 18:17; 1 Cor 6:5; Ex 18:16 selves. They should lead the community spiritually in its response to the word of the Lord and
call the members of the community on to holiness
of life and selfless love. They should do all these
things, not necessarily by being in a counseling
relationship with each member of the community,
but as shepherds leading the group and directly
1 Pt 5:2-4 encouraging and correcting each member.

1 Tm 5:17 As laborers for the Lord, elders should work to
build up and feed the body, especially by teaching
and preaching. They should not serve in such a
way as to take away from others their initiative in
building the body up; rather their work should
encourage others to take active responsibility.
Nonetheless, they should actively labor to build
up the body as they fulfill their responsibility to
watch over and shepherd the community.

Jn 10:11 The elders need the heart of a shepherd. They
should love to see each person grow strong and
1 Thes 2:11-12 happy in the Lord. They should represent and act
in the love of the good shepherd. In their love,

they should neglect neither compassion nor discipline, but they should faithfully provide for each one what that person needs to grow strong. 1 Thes 5:12-14

## *6. Selecting elders*

Choosing elders is one of the most serious tasks that communities undertake, and they should be ready to devote themselves to it seriously. Finding the right men to be elders is one of the greatest keys to the well-being of community. The choice of new elders is primarily entrusted to the body of elders, subject to any higher governing authorities. The body of elders or those within it who have the primary responsibility for the choice should not accept someone whose life they do not know well, nor should they accept someone they have not worked with for a period of time in building up the body. The whole community, moreover, should have a significant voice in determining who should be considered for elder. Finally, the person who is chosen as elder should be at peace with being chosen and should be satisfied that his serving as elder is pleasing to the Lord. Elders should not be elected by relying on some procedure, but they should be chosen by approval of the other elders based on knowledge of the man and his gifts, with the general acceptance of the community.

Elders should be mature Christian men who are capable of bearing responsibility for the whole community. They should be solid in their commitment to the Lord and in their faith in him. They should be eager in their obedience to him and to his word. They should be formed in Christian character and experienced in their abil-

1 Tm 3:1-7; Ti 1:5-11; Rom 12:3-8

ity to handle the different situations of life in a
Christian manner. They should have training in
the scripture and Christian teaching, especially in
2 Tm 2:2, 3:10-17 all matters they will have to handle as an elder.
They should be free from serious faults and not
under the control of drink, money, fear or anger.
They should be the kind of men whom others
readily respect. They should be reliable in responsibilities that are entrusted to them. Their word
1 Tm 2:12 should be good. They should be men, not women.
They should normally be among the older men in
age and Christian experience of those in the
community. They should have given evidence of a
gift for governing others, especially their own
households. They should be trained in handling
their responsibilities as elders. They should be
able to teach others. They should be free from
arrogance and the desire to dominate, but should
be ready to serve and work hard. They should love
the Lord and his people.

Elders should be chosen because they are the ones who are the spiritually natural ones to govern the community. Being an elder is not a reward for virtue or faithful service, nor is it a promotion. Elders should not be chosen out of fear or expedience, but they should be chosen because the body and its governors are convinced that the Lord has gifted someone to be an elder, and the right time has come for him to assume that position.

## 7. *Ceasing to be an elder*

Elders are not chosen for a term of office, but they are chosen for as long as it seems right in the Lord for them to serve as elders. They should serve until they are no longer needed or are no longer capable of serving well. Elders should not be deposed unless they fall into serious sin or violate community order in a serious way. If they 1 Tm 5:19-22 are unable to uphold important directions of the community that have been properly agreed upon, they can be required to resign by the body of elders, but they should not be required to resign for simply disagreeing with the direction or for dissenting in good order. An elder can also be asked to resign by the body of elders or by some group of elders responsible for his service, if for reasons of health, age, or personal circumstances or for reasons of practical advantage to the body (such as lack of need for so many elders) it would be good for him or for the community for there to be a change. He would do well to accept the request especially if there is a consensus among the body of elders. An elder can be required to resign or retire for the above reasons by a consensus of the remainder of the body of elders if these reasons prevent him from fulfilling his responsibilities.

## *8. Servants and handmaids*

Servants and handmaids shall be chosen to as- 1 Tm 3:8-13 sist the elders in their government of the community. They serve as the extensions of the elders and allow the elders to have a more effective care for the whole life of the body. The servants will especially have care of the material and administrative aspects of the government of the community, but they shall be available for any service the elders entrust to them. The handmaids will especially have care for the women and the needy in the community, but they too shall be available for any need. Both will work closely under the elders of the community, and will not view their service as being independent of the service of the body of elders. Both will be chosen for maturity of Christian life and ability to perform the services they will be given. They should be people who can be respected as leaders in the community.

### *9. The spirit of service*

Lk 22:24-27; Mt 18:1-4; 1 Cor 3:5; 1 Pt 5:2-3

Those who serve as governors of the community should never domineer others or rule for their own benefit. They are appointed to be servants, following the example of their Lord Jesus. That does not mean that they should not exercise authority firmly, nor that what they do will always be

Ti 1:13, 3:8-10

pleasing to those under them. But nonetheless, they are appointed as servants to serve the members of the household of God. They do not hold positions of responsibility for their own benefit, but in order to build up the body. They should approach those under them respectfully, with a readiness to lay down their lives or to perform any service. Yet, those under them are not their masters, but the Lord himself. He is the one who directs their service. He is the one who is responsible for giving the increase.

## *Notes:*

a. This section is written to be compatible with a variety of structures of government. It allows for the community to be under a higher governing body or not to be. It allows for the body of elders to have more or less authority relative to the community. It does not, however, allow for the community as a whole to have the final directive authority nor to have the final decision as to who should be the elder, although it does allow for the community to have a voice in directing itself and to choose elders from a body of men chosen by the elders or to elect a presiding elder from among the body of elders. The statement allows the presiding elder to be more of a chief pastor and for the other elders to be clearly subordinate to him, and it allows for him to be more of a moderator of the body. It does not, however, allow for an independently functioning presiding elder, unchecked by others, or for an ungoverned body of elders. The statement that the body of elders is the highest governing authority has to be seen in light of the variation allowed by this section. This statement needs to be supplemented by further decisions.

b. The statement is written to allow the presiding elder or the body of elders to be the final authority in decision-making, though not to allow the presiding elder to make major decisions without the other elders having a chance to openly counsel him. It is written to allow the presiding elder or the body of elders to appoint elders to positions of responsibility, but not to allow any elder to serve unsupervised. It is written to allow the presiding elder or some group of elders to be the court of appeal from the decision of an elder, although rules of judicial procedure would indicate that the elder in question should never be part of the body hearing an appeal from his action and that the presiding elder should not decide on major matters alone. The statement is written to allow for the body of elders to have final authority in any review of the work of the presiding elder, but not to require it. It is not, however, written to allow the presiding elder to serve free of the possibility of all review. It is written to allow the presiding elder to be under the authority of some of the elders in his personal life and service or to simply be under their counsel, but it is not written to allow him to be free of ongoing care by other elders in the local community.

c. The statement is written for groups which accept the Christian scriptures (the Old and New Testament) as the final authority not to be contradicted. It does not rule out adding the role of tradition and of authoritative church decisions (canons of councils, creeds, confessions, etc.).

d. The constitution of the community refers to the covenant of the community if there is one, to this statement if it is so adopted, and to any other set of decisions which determine the basic shape and order of the community and which cannot be changed by elders in their normal functioning, either because they are given by an authority recognized as being over the body of elders or because they are protected and can only be changed in accordance with special procedures.

# IV. Peace and Discipline

## *1. The commitment to holiness and righteousness*

Holiness and righteousness should characterize the life of every body of Christians. God is holy, and his people should live lives of holiness. They should imitate the Lord Jesus and have his character formed in them, so that they may be suitable dwelling places for the Holy Spirit. A Christian community cannot allow sin and wrongdoing to be an accepted part of the lives of its members, nor can it allow a lack of love and peace to be an accepted part of its life together. If a body of Christians does not follow the way of life that Jesus taught, it cannot function as his body in the world.

Eph 4:22-24
1 Pt 1:14-16; Lv 19:1-2
Eph 5:1-2; Gal 4:19; Eph 2:21-22
1 Cor 1:10-11, 3:1-4, 5:6-8; 2 Cor 12:20-21; 2 Pt 3:14; Mt 5:13-14

A community of Christians is called to holiness together as a body and not just individually. The way individual Christians live their lives is not a private matter solely between them and God. They have made a commitment to one another to obey the Lord and follow his ways. Moreover, when a group of Christians is a body together, the sin of one is harmful to the others. One person's sin can block the action of God in the body and can affect the spiritual health of other members of the

1 Pt 2:4,9
Dt 29:8-12; Jos 24: 19-24; 2 Chr 15:10-15, 23:16
Jos 7:10-26; Acts 5:1-11; 1 Cor 5:6

body and of the body as a whole. Living a life that is righteous and loving builds the body up, while living unrighteously weakens it and sometimes damages it.

The members of a Christian community are responsible for one another's lives. Since they belong to one another and depend on one another as members of the same body, they are account-
Rom 12:5 able to one another for the way they live. Since they have made a commitment together to follow the Lord, they can call one another to be faithful to
Col 3:16 that commitment. Since they are brothers and sisters bound together in love, they have to care for one another in their weakness and sin as much as
1 Jn 1:7; Jn 3:21; in any other condition of need. The members of a
Eph 5:11 Christian community should not reserve parts of their lives for themselves as if they were independent units, unconnected to the body. They should be responsible for one another with love, caring for one another as they would wish to be cared for.

## *2. Mutual encouragement and correction*

The members of a body are responsible for helping one another grow in the life of the Lord. The Lord has called Christians to encourage one
1 Thes 5:11; Col 3:16; another and build one another up. They should be
Rom 1:11-12 engaged in a constant process of strengthening one another, calling one another on, passing on what the Lord has taught, and in every way helping one another's growth in love and faithfulness to the Lord. Such personal help should normally be given in a spirit of encouragement and of rejoicing in one another, and not in a spirit of
1 Cor 1:4-17 dissatisfaction and criticism. It should be part of a
Phil 1:8-11 life of ongoing kindness and thankfulness for one another. Members of a body of Christians should

normally like to be with one another. Ps(s) 16:3, 133

At the same time, Christians occasionally fail in righteousness or in faithfulness to their commitments. Sometimes such wrongdoing is serious. Even the strongest Christians have to take heed lest they fall. Sometimes the wrongdoing is light. Even the truly righteous person sins in this sense. In all cases of wrongdoing, the primary responsibility for correcting the wrong belongs to those who have done the wrong. They should repent, confess their wrongdoings to the Lord (and to others when appropriate) and if possible make up for what they have done. When the wrongdoing is serious, they should be especially earnest to change so that such wrongdoing never occurs again.

1 Cor 10:12; Phil 2:12; Prv 24:16

Lv 5:5; Nm 5:17; Ps 32: 3-5; Lk 18:9-14, 19:1-9; 1 Jn 1:9

Lk 3:8; 2 Cor 7:9-11

But the responsibility for someone's wrongdoing also belongs to the others in the community. Wrongdoing that has not yet been repented of becomes the concern of others. Wrongdoing should normally be corrected by a direct admonition, reproof, or even rebuke. Sometimes correction should involve punishment. Correction should be given lovingly and in a spirit of respect, directly and simply. Those who are receiving correction should receive it eagerly and thankfully. They should desire to see all wrongdoing removed from their life, and to be molded in the image of Christ, worthy temples of the Holy Spirit. They should not desire to defend themselves or to hide their wrongdoing. Instead they should want to have what is wrong exposed and changed. They should receive correction with patience, patience toward their own weaknesses and toward the failings of their brothers and sisters who correct them, and they should receive

Lk 17:3; Col 3:13; Eph 5:11; 2 Cor 2:6

Rv 3:19; Gal 6:1; 2 Tm 2:25; Ps 141:5; Prv 25:12 Prv 9:7-9, 12:1, 27:5-6

it with full faith and hope in God and in his power
Heb 12:11 to change them and make them new.

There are other types of correction than for wrongdoing. Correction can often be given to help someone improve in an area where he is already free from wrongdoing. Correction can also be given to help someone learn to work better or to acquire some skill. In these cases, correction should be given and received in the same spirit as correction for wrongdoing, but correction for improvement in Christian living or for learning a skill does not call for confession of wrongdoing or asking for forgiveness.

Members of a Christian community are not
obligated to correct everything that is wrong.
More often they are called to bear with their
Eph 4:2; Col 3:13; brothers and sisters and with their failings. There
1 Cor 13:7 are times when Christians are responsible to give
correction, and at those times they must not avoid
the task, even if it should be very difficult or seem
Prv 13:24, 23:13, 27:5 like it will be fruitless. But for the rest, the
guidelines for giving correction should be whether
the correction will be helpful to others at this time.
When it is not helpful, we should wait patiently,
showing the same forbearance to others that the
Lord shows to us.

## *3. Peace in the body*

Mt 22:37-40; Eph 4:3 Christians should be at peace with one another.
The presence of the Holy Spirit in their midst
should bring the peace that comes from God, the
peace that is based on a right relationship with
God and a genuine commitment to love one
Rom 5:1-5; another. It is a peace that is based on obedience to
1 Jn 5:2-3, 4:21 God and his commandments. God's command-

ments are not a statement of the rights that we can demand from one another. Rather they are a revelation of how the Lord wants his people to live together and to serve one another. They reveal how he intends life to be lived among his people, and his people should obey them as such. Within a Christian community there should be a harmony that results from the obedience of the brothers and sisters to the righteousness taught by God for their lives. Rom 15:5-6

A Christian community should be free from conflict, hostility, grudges, resentment, and bitterness. Each member of the body should be at peace with every other member of the body. When members of the community know that there is something wrong in their relationship with another community member, whether they have something against the other or the other has something against them, they should go and seek reconciliation. And they should not rest until reconciliation has been achieved. Moreover, they should guard their hearts from resentment, hidden suspicions, personal anger, and anything that might give rise to hatred or hostility towards a brother or sister. One of the most serious obligations that comes from belonging to the body of Christ is the obligation of preserving peace with other members of the body.

1 Cor 3:1-4; Gal 5:15, 25-26; 1 Thes 5:13

Mt 5:23-24; 18:15

Eph 4:31; Col 3:8

Sometimes two members of the community are unable to work out a dispute between them. In such a case, they should go to someone with governing authority in the community for a judgment. When brothers and sisters in the Lord seek a judgment, they should go seeking wisdom on how this particular difficulty should be resolved according to the intention of the Lord for

1 Cor 6:1-7; Dt 17:8-11

this area of their lives. They should not be
concerned with defending their own rights or
being vindicated, but should seek the greatest
good of the body. They should prefer to be
defrauded rather than to harm another member of
the body or cause dissension in the body as a
1 Cor 6:7-8 whole. Members of a Christian community should
normally not go to the secular courts for judgment
in something involving other members of the
community, for they thereby seek the power to get
their own way rather than wisdom about God's
1 Cor 6:1-6 way.

Conflicts between members of the body are the
responsibility of the whole body. When a conflict
arises, each person who has the opportunity
should urge the disputants to quickly resolve the
Phil 4:2-3 conflict in peace. Stirring up quarrels or saying
things that will cause people to mistrust or be
resentful towards one another are serious forms of
wrongdoing, and the community should guard
itself against such actions as much as against actual
Prv 6:19, 16:28, conflicts. The whole body should insist upon
18:8, 26:20 peace and trust. In Christ there is no quarrel that
cannot be resolved. The reign of Christ is a reign
Rom 14:17 of peace, joy, and righteousness in the Holy Spirit.

## *4. Government and discipline*

Discipline among the Christian people is entrusted to individual Christians according to the responsibility they have for the lives of others. Those who have a governing authority in the Christian community have been given a direct responsibility for the discipline of others in the community within the limits of what has been entrusted to them to govern. The elders have been given the commission to watch over the life of the whole community and the lives of all who belong to the community. They have therefore been entrusted with the responsibility for the discipline of the whole community. Others have a governing authority for some portion of the community as do, for instance, fathers of families, and they have a responsibility for discipline within that portion of the community under the overall responsibility of the elders.

1 Thes 5:12-14; 2 Tm 3:16-17, 4:2; 2 Cor 13:1-4; 1 Cor 4:18-21

Prv 13:24, 23:13

The governing authority which is given to different members of the community is primarily an authority to build up in the Lord those who are in their care. Those with governing authority are entrusted with the responsibility of leading those they care for to lives of deeper holiness and greater love for God and one another. They are therefore called to work on behalf of those in their care, feeding them with Christian teaching, and providing them with the help they need to grow in the Christian life. At the same time, the Lord has entrusted to those responsible for governing in a Christian community a responsibility for the peace and discipline of the body, and an authority that corresponds to their responsibility. It is their responsibility to settle disputes in the body and to correct individuals within the body. They have, in other words, the competency to judge within their area of governmental responsibility. They can therefore give decisions which are authoritative and correct individuals authoritatively subject to any higher authorities in the Lord.

1 Cor 3:5-9, 21-23; 2 Cor 10:8

2 Cor 13:10

1 Cor 5: Ti 1:5,11; 2:15; Dt 17:8-13

Governors should take an ongoing responsibility for the discipline of those in their care. They should always correct whatever is seriously out of order, whether it be major wrongdoing,

significant failure to fulfill responsibility, or significant difficulties or problems in personal Chris-
Heb 13:7 tian living. Beyond handling matters that are seriously out of order, they should seek to provide any personal care that may be helpful in leading others to a fuller holiness and righteousness in Christian living. They should not burden people by calling for too much or by correcting too severely or too often, but they can and often should call on those who are ready for more. They should be conscious of the differences among those in their care and handle each person appropriately.

The members of the community are committed to respect and honor their governors in the community as people who have been set over them
1 Thes 5:12-13 in the Lord. Out of reverence for the Lord, they are responsible to receive what is being given to
Eph 5:21 them. They should be eager to receive the teaching, admonition, or exhortation of their governors, both when it is given to the whole group they are part of and when it is given to them personally. They should receive a personal reproof or judgment by their governor as something that they are committed to accept, and either obey it or, if they have a serious reservation, appeal to the governor who is over their governor. They are also committed to love their governors as brothers and sisters who serve them and who often have a
1 Thes 5:13; Heb 13:17; Gal 6:6 difficult service. They should respond to them willingly and with a thankfulness for the help they are being given.

### 5. *Serious wrongdoing*

Occasionally members of a community do not respond to normal correction. If the matter involves serious wrongdoing, or if someone refuses to be reconciled with another member of the community, or if there is a pattern of regular disorders or significant ongoing difficulties in someone's Christian life in the community, if, in other words, the matter is serious, it becomes the responsibility of the elders of the body. The elders should not pass over any serious matter that has been brought to their attention, but should investigate it and either clear the person or discipline him. Serious sin is a danger to the spiritual welfare of both the community and the individual who sinned. Moreover, among those who believe in the word of the Lord, it is a great failure in love to leave someone in his sin or let him experience a false peace in his life. The elders will have to give an account for every failure to deal adequately with things that are seriously wrong.

Dt 16:18-20, 19:15-21, 17:9; Mt 18:16-17

Prv 24:23-25; 1 Cor 5:2,6; 2 Cor 12:20-13:4; Rv 2:14-16, 19-21

Heb 13:17

When a matter involving serious wrongdoing comes to the attention of the elders and those involved do not acknowledge they have done any wrong, the elders should carefully investigate the matter. The matter can begin with a charge by a community member or an elder with governing authority whose correction or judgment is not being accepted. The matter can also begin with community members who wish to clear their reputation when it is being endangered. Three elders should be appointed to act as judges of the case, not including the elder who brings the charge if the case originates with him. The judges should be competent, impartial and not involved in the matter. They should provide a fair trial before coming to a judgment. They should hear both sides, confront the accuser with the accused, accept no evidence on the basis of only one witness or on the basis of a witness lacking in credibility,

Dt 17:4, 19:18; Lv 5:1, 19:15-18; 2 Cor 12:20-13:4

Dt 19:17

Dt 19:15-21; Prv 18:17; Dt 17:2-7; 2 Cor 13:1; Mt 18:15-20

Lv 5:1

Dt 17:8-9

and decide only after all the testimony is taken. They should conduct the trial without prejudice or partiality towards any party. Community members are obligated to support the trial by giving testimony when that is needed. If the case is too difficult the judges should refer it to those with greater competence. Judgments can be appealed if there are good grounds for believing that justice might not have been done. Providing true justice in matters of serious wrongdoing is one of the more important responsibilities of the elders to the Lord and to the community members.

2 Sam 23:2-3; 1 Kgs 3:28; Prv 18:5, 28:5, 29:4; 1 Cor 5:1-8

Prv 17:10; Lk 12:46-48; Mt 18:8-9; 1 Cor 5:1-2; 2 Cor 2:5-11, 13:10

Lk 17:3; 2 Tm 4:2; Ti 1:13

Ti 3:10-11

2 Cor 2:5-11; 2 Thes 3:14-15 Mt 18:17; 1 Cor 5:3-5; 1 Tm 1:20; Gal 1:8-9; 2 Cor 12:20-13:4; Rv 2:19-21

How the elders deal with those who have committed serious wrongdoing varies with the situation. Sometimes the main concern is to bring people to a genuine change of heart. Sometimes people have repented and the concern is to change and restore them so that they will not fall into the same difficulty in the future. A remedy should be used that is fitting and appropriate to the problem. It is a disservice to the person and a failure before the Lord to treat something too lightly or to treat something too severely. Discipline begins with normal correction. It can make use of solemn reproof and rebuke either in private or before others. It can involve special disciplinary treatment of the person by his or her governor, such as curtailment of normal privileges in the community and exclusion from participation in some community activities, or personal avoidance. It could also involve special treatment of the person by the community as a whole, usually some form of avoidance. Finally, for matters of great enough seriousness, it can involve exclusion. In all these matters the discipline used should not be used for revenge, but with a desire to save and heal without compromising the truth. The person should understand clearly that the various measures are being taken for discipline and involve no personal rejection. For many this will involve an education in the significance of Christian discipline and in how it can be exercised with love and respect. The process of discipline should not become public except as a deliberate step when the matter has become so serious that it is appropriate for the body as a whole to be involved.

1 Cor 5:3-5

Exclusion is a severe Christian discipline, and is a matter of great seriousness. It is used primarily for wrongdoings which disqualify a person from inheritance in the kingdom of Christ. These include violations of the basic moral commandments such as murder, adultery, sexual immorality, homosexuality, robbery, greed, and being a drunkard, as well as persistence in enmity toward a brother or sister, publicly professing opinions incompatible with basic Christian truths, participating in non-Christian worship and engaging in the occult, spiritualism, or any other activity which involves conscious relationships with unholy spirits (including so-called neutral spirits). Exclusion can also follow upon serious refusal to abide by community order, for an attack on the order of a body is a threat to its life.

1 Cor 5:11, 6:9-10;
Eph 5:5; Rv 21:8

1 Tm 1:20;
Gal 1:8-9;
Rv 2:14-16

Rv 2:20-24

Ti 3:10-11

Exclusion should involve careful investigation and decision. It is used to bring someone to repentance and as a remedy. It has to be done with some involvement of the body as a whole, because of its very nature. People can only return to full participation in the life of the community after some remedial process designed to restore them and reestablish them in full Christian

1 Cor 5:3-5;
2 Cor 2:5-11
Rom 16:17;
1 Cor 5:9-11;
2 Jn 10; Mt 18:17

Christian strength. Exclusion is not the same as terminating a relationship with someone who has dropped away or lost his commitment. It is a disciplinary action against the members of the body for matters that constitute a crime before the Lord and it is based on the recognition that a good standing has already been broken by the wrong-doing itself.

For those who have a responsibility in the Lord
for the lives of others, all exercise of discipline
should be done in a way that is appropriate to a
shepherd. The shepherd must watch over the
whole flock, and often must protect it against
Ez 34:8, 11-16; Acts 20:28-30 harm that comes from one of the sheep. But the
shepherd also cares for each sheep in love, and his
Ez 34:16; Mt 18:10-14; Jas 5:19-20 desire is to save each one. Discipline within a
Christian community is a manifestation of the love
with which the Lord trains and disciplines us.
Ti 2:11-14 Spiritual discipline is not a matter of meting out a
specific punishment. Rather it is a work of spiri-
Mt 18:15; Gal 6:1 tual preservation and restoration. It should not
cease until the person has been fully restored to a
loving relationship with brothers and sisters in the
Lord.

## *6. Discipline of elders*

The elders of a Christian community also need
the protection of Christian discipline. Because of
their responsibility they are held accountable in a
greater way by the Lord, yet at the same time they
are exposed to special opportunities for wrong-
Jer 10:21, 23:1-6; Ez 34:1-6; Zc 11:15-17 doing in connection with their position. Elders can
fall into using their authority for personal gain or
advantage or using their position to dominate
Is 3:14-15, 10:1-4 rather than serve others. They can be guilty of
injustice in judgment and discipline, false teach-

ing, or any of the abuses to which spiritual authority can become prey. They can violate community order or act in an insubordinate way. The very respect due to an elder can prevent others from having the courage to correct him before he commits serious wrongdoing or discipline him while he can still be saved. The position of the elders as men who are over the rest of the community means that there is a need for a special approach to their discipline.

Jer 22:1-10; Dt 17:18-20; 2 Chr 9-10; Acts 20:28-30 3 Jn 9-10

1 Kgs 22:13-23; 1 Tm 5: 20-21

Elders can be admonished by those who are under them if the admonition is given respectfully. They will normally receive much helpful correction from their brother-elders. But the main responsibility for the correction of an elder belongs to the presiding elder or to whomever the presiding elder has designated responsibility for the elder in question. If an elder has not accepted correction given in a serious manner and the person who has corrected him does not see that it is right to let the matter go, he should present the situation to the presiding elder or his delegate.

1 Tm 5:19-22

The elder should receive a fair trial as outlined in Section 5. The presiding elder should appoint judges for the trial. If there are not enough elders in the community who are competent or who are not involved in the matter, he should refer the case to a higher authority or should find men who can be competent judges. He should also allow appeal if questions arise as to the justice of the trial.[a]

Censure of elders will normally be conducted within the body of elders. Solemn rebuke before the body of elders by the presiding elder is one particularly severe disciplinary action. In cases of actions which merit exclusion for an ordinary

1 Tm 5:20

community member, public deposition from
being an elder can be as severe a disciplinary
action as public exclusion for an ordinary member,
although a deposed elder who continues in serious
sin cannot be allowed to remain as part of the life
1 Tm 5:19 of the body. The discipline of an elder is a matter
of great seriousness for a community, and failure
to exercise this discipline is itself a serious wrong-
1 Tm 5:21-22 doing on the part of those responsible. Those who
discipline an elder should do so with care and
respect for him and his position, but they should
1 Tm 5:21 be determined to avoid partiality or fear.

Is 3:12-14, 10:1; Jer 5:30-31 There can come a time when the body of elders
as a whole either falls into serious wrongdoing in
its exercise of authority in the community, or
habitually condones serious wrongdoing among
the elders or in the body as a whole. Members of
the community who see such wrongdoing can
reprove the body of elders, either individually or
joined together with a few of the more mature and
wise among the brothers in the community. If
their reproof is not received, they can appeal for
help to whatever authority there may be that is
over the community. In all their concern, they
should entrust the situation to the judgment and
action of the Lord who is capable of watching over
Jer 22:13-23; Is 3:14 his people. The prayer of a righteous man has
Jas 5:16-18 great power in its effects.

## 7. *The responsibility of community members*

Every Christian bears some responsibility for the life of others in the community and, therefore, for their discipline. Sometimes it is a direct responsibility that comes from a position of governance such as the responsibility of parents for their children, or the responsibility of a man for whomever he takes into his house as a member of the household, or the responsibility of the elders or of any other governing authorities in the community.

In addition, members of the community have a fraternal responsibility for one another. As brothers and sisters in the Lord, they build one another up in the Lord and call one another to lives of holiness and righteousness. This responsibility is normally exercised in sharing, teaching, admonition, encouragement, and exhortation, but it can also be exercised in reproof or rebuke. Because it is a genuine responsibility, it carries authority with it. When a brother or sister in the Lord seriously and deliberately speaks a word of exhortation or admonition, a person's first response should be to accept the word. People can sometimes legitimately put aside serious correction given them by a brother or sister in the Lord, but they should not do so lightly and normally should not do so without the counsel of someone who is over them in the Lord.

1 Thes 5:11; Col 3:13

Members of the community have a fraternal responsibility for all other members of the Christian community. However, brothers and sisters should carry out that responsibility differently with those who are near to them, with whom they share their lives in some ongoing way, than with those who are more distant from them. Whenever they can show their love or give encouragement or share some wisdom with another member of the body, they should do so. Normally, however, they should not correct someone they are not close to, unless they are sure that they fully understand the situation and are confident that they can give the correction in a way that will be helpful. Correction is most successfully given when set in the context of a loving personal relationship.

Fraternal responsibility involves a direct responsibility for one's own personal difficulties with other members of the community. When brothers or sisters are personally wronged by another brother or sister, they should repair the relationship by going to the person who has wronged them, inquiring about the matter, and perhaps speaking a word of reproof directly to him. If the reproof is not accepted, and the matter is serious, the next step is to lay the matter before the responsible governor, normally an elder. When the matter is not serious, it can be passed over and the wrong endured.

Mt 18:15-17

Lv 5:1; Prv 29:24

Fraternal responsibility also involves a direct responsibility when a brother or sister witnesses a serious wrongdoing committed by another brother or sister, or recognizes something seriously out of order in their life. If someone with governing authority over the brother or sister who committed a serious wrong is also a witness, he has the direct responsibility, but in other cases the fraternal relationship involves having a direct responsibility. Normally when members of the community are aware of some serious wrong, they should speak about it to the person first and then lay the matter before an elder, but sometimes they should go to the elder first. When they present something to an elder, they should always be ready to be identified and to be called upon to speak with their brother or sister about what they have observed.

When serious wrongdoing comes to the attention of members of the community, but they are

not a personal witness to it, they have a fraternal but not direct responsibility for the welfare of their brother or sister, unless they have governmental responsibility for the person involved. Because the responsibility is not a direct one, they should not personally investigate the matter, but should communicate to the responsible elder that there might be something which demands attention and suggest that he investigate further. The Dt 19:18
elder might communicate back to them, but if not, they should forget the matter and hold no suspicions of their brother or sister, assuming that the information they received was incorrect unless they know for sure otherwise.

## *8. Responsibility outside the community*

Christians do not have the same kind of responsibility for those who are not part of the Christian community that they do for their brothers and sisters in the Lord. Their responsibility for non-Christians does not include a disciplinary responsibility, except when they have been given a position by the secular society that involves disciplinary responsibility (if they are, for instance, governmental officials or employers), and in these instances should not expect to be able to use the ways of the Christian community in exercising authority outside the Christian community. When 1 Cor 5:12-13
Christians see something seriously wrong in the life of a non-Christian, they should normally pass it by. Those who are not in the Lord will normally 1 Thes 4:11-12
have serious wrongdoing in their lives. However, Ti 3:3-8
Christians are responsible for serving non-Christians with the mercy of the heavenly Father. Lk 6:32-36; Ti 3:4-8
They should present the good news of salvation to non-Christians so that they can be brought to a

position of freedom and truth where they can be expected to live a righteous life. If Christians can serve non-Christians by telling them the truth about their life or by encouraging them to live more in accordance with what God has taught, they should do so, but they should take care that they do not make the non-Christians less open to the gospel, which is the hope of salvation, by being judgmental. Christians should love non-Christians, just as God loves the world, but they should not relate to them as if they were responsible for them as for their brothers and sisters in the Lord.

Col 4:5-6
Jn 3:16-18

## *9. Speech and wrongdoing*

Jas 3:1-10; Prv 18:21

Peace can exist within the body of Christ and discipline carried out in a loving way only if the body as a whole guards its speech carefully. The tongue is a great means of loving service. Its true call is to glorify God and build up the brothers and sisters. But it can also be very destructive. Speaking against others, judging others, gossiping against others, criticizing others, or abusing others can sow mistrust and dissension in a community and destroy its ability to be a community of love. When discipline of the tongue is preserved, however, the way in which brothers and sisters speak to one another can be one of the greatest sources of love in the community.

Ps 34:1-3; Phil 4:8;
Prv 11:9

The Christian community as a whole is not normally a court. The community can become a court when gathering in solemn assembly under the presidency of its elders on special occasions, but the daily life of a community is not a court. In some groups the whole people together is a court, and charges against individuals, especially public

1 Cor 5:4-5

officials, are made in a public way by whomever chooses to make them. But in the body of Christ, matters of judgment are handled differently. Only certain members of the body, those with governing authority, are given responsibility for judgment and discipline, and only the elders have the responsibility for the judgment and discipline of the whole body. Accusations should never be made except to those with responsibility for the person accused. Investigations should not be carried out except by the person with responsibility. People's difficulties should not be discussed except with someone who has governmental responsibility for the person with the difficulties. The only individuals it is permissible to speak with about wrongdoing and difficulties in another person's life are those who are directly responsible for that person and who are committed to care for the person.

Mt 7:1; 1 Cor 5:2,5

Christians should not speak against one another or against any person, even if what they are saying is true. To speak against another is to act as a judge. Nor should they gossip, passing on reports against someone, stirring up suspicion and mistrust against a brother or sister. If they observe something wrong, they should either speak to the person or to someone responsible for the person, and they should do it in the proper way. If they are uncertain how to handle a matter, they can ask counsel, but they should ask counsel from someone who has governing responsibility in the body. If they are asked by someone who has governing responsibility, they can give that person the information in their possession. Those who are in positions of authority should never speak against a member of the body or anyone else openly, unless

2 Cor 12:20; 1 Pt 2:1; Rom 1:30; 2 Tm 3:3; Ti 2:3

Jas 4:11; Mt 7:1

2 Cor 12:20; 1 Tm 5:13; Lv 19:16; Prv 11:13, 16:28, 20:19

they have to warn the body against that person or unless they are involved in public discipline of that person. No one should speak against another Christian unless he has a responsibility to do so.

Members of a Christian body should not believe accusations unless they personally know them to be true. When they hear accusations, they should only entertain them if the accusations concern someone they are responsible for. Then they should investigate the accusation to see if it is true before believing it. They should expect the person presenting the accusation to take part openly in the investigation, and they should not allow themselves to be bound to confidentiality. When they hear accusations about people that they are
Prv 17:4 not responsible for, they should not receive them. They should themselves forget the accusations and not allow suspicions to be sown in their hearts. They should also correct brothers and sisters who have not presented the accusation to the right person and when possible they should refuse to listen to accusations or gossip.

1 Pt 4:15 Christians should never feel called upon to be curious about how brothers or sisters are living their lives nor to investigate reports or evidences of wrongdoing or serious difficulties, unless they have governmental responsibility for that person. They should entrust all concern or investigation to those who are responsible for the person and only take a concern for situations they are directly involved in. Fraternal responsibility is direct only when there is a personal involvement in the difficulty, either as a direct witness or as a party in a dispute.

Members of the body of Christ should not give negative evaluations (criticisms) of how others conduct their services and duties unless they are responsible to do so. Then they should only do so to someone who is over the person concerned or the particular service the person is discharging. They are free to evaluate openly how well activities, jobs or services go, but they should not openly give an evaluative judgment of how people discharge their services and duties. Even when there is no wrongdoing involved, they are not free to evaluate the people, because that involves taking a responsibility in speech for someone that they do not have responsibility for.

Finally, members of the body of Christ should never insult or abuse anyone. To attack someone with the tongue is equivalent to attacking him physically and is something more harmful. There should be peace and not conflict within a Christian community, and Christians should aim to be peacemakers for those who are not part of the Christian community.

Mt 5:19; 1 Cor 5:11; Eph 4:31; Col 3:8; 1 Tm 6:4; 2 Tm 3:2 Rom 12:18, Ti 3:2; 1 Pt 3:9

## *10. True holiness and righteousness*

Gal 5:13; Rom 6:15-19

The commitment together of a body of Christians to holiness and righteousness in their daily lives can be a great source of freedom because it can provide power for each member of that body to live as a son or daughter of God. Such a commitment can also lead to a deep experience of brotherly love and a sense of security that comes through a confidence in the care of brothers and sisters. The dedication of a body of Christians to help one another live the kind of life they are committed to can be a great protection against sin and personal failure in Christian living. When Christians live a common commitment to holiness and righteousness and when they live that com-

mitment in the Holy Spirit, the commitment will
be one of freedom and love, a joyful commitment.
When Christians slip away from the Spirit and
from an inner commitment of their heart and fall
into an observance of the law only, the commitment will simply lead to mutual surveillance and
Rom 7:6, 13:8; social pressure. Community in holiness and righ-
1 Tm 1:8-10; teousness is so central to the nature of the
Gal 5:25 Christian call that it cannot be approached except
by the power of the Holy Spirit.

The goal which the Lord sets before his people
is not simply to keep the rules correctly. The goal
which the Lord sets before his people is that pure
love of God and neighbor which is a reflection of
Mt 22:37-39 his own divine nature. The goal is that God's own
image be fashioned in the life of his people as a
Col 3:10 whole and in the lives of each of his followers.
Through the Holy Spirit, the Lord wishes to teach
his people the wisdom that will let them see the
Col 1:9-10, 2:2-3 goal with greater and greater clarity. Then they
will be able to apply laws and ordinances and rules
and teachings as tools which help a heart that is set
Rom 6:17 on the Lord to follow his ways. Then they will be
able to help one another use the same tools to
strengthen the life of the Lord that is in them.

Above all else, Christians have to hold unfail-
1 Pt 4:8 ingly their love for one another. They are
responsible for the lives of one another, but that
responsibility should be exercised with loving
care, with respect and compassion. When Christians care for one another as they want to be cared
for themselves, then they have heard the message
Mt 7:12 of the law and the prophets.

# *Notes:*

a. The discipline of the presiding elder is not covered in the statement. Every community needs a procedure for such a situation. If at all possible, final authority for the discipline of the presiding elder should lie outside the local community.

# V. Government and Personal Direction[a]

## 1. Government of people in a Christian community

Those who belong to a Christian community are subject to its governmental authority for their whole lives. This authority arises out of the nature of the commitment involved in being a Christian community. Members of a Christian community have committed more than just some of their time and resources. They have committed their whole lives to the Lord and to one another. The government of the community therefore extends to everything in their lives. Moreover, a Christian community should be able to serve the Lord as a body. The community must be able to act effectively as a unit, and lives of the members of the community must be interdependent. Therefore, there must be an authority in the community which is able to govern the body as a whole and the individual members.

Acts 2:44, 4:32

Rom 12:3-5; 1 Cor 12:12-27

Elders and those under them who exercise the governing authority of the community lead and care for the body and its members. They govern the community by teaching, correcting, disciplining, encouraging and building up the community, and they can do so with authority. In addition, they govern the community by directing the

2 Tm 4:2; Ti 2:15

Heb 13:17; 1 Tm 3:5, 5:17; 1 Pt 5:5; 1 Cor 16:16

community and its members. Their authority to direct, when used wisely and in obedience to the Lord, is one of the greater sources of power belonging to the body.

## *2. Personal direction and all community members*

Many relationships within a Christian community involve personal subordination. The exercise of authority in those relationships varies depending on the purpose of the relationship. Therefore, the kind of direction which the governing authority gives also varies according to the relationship.

Acts 14:23, 20:28; 1 Thes 5: 12-13; Heb 13:17; 1 Pt 5:1-5

Overall authority within the Christian community belongs to the body of elders under the presiding elder of the community. Elders have a responsibility to watch over and care for all the members of the community, to see that each person's life goes well, that everyone is being formed in the image of Christ, and that all find their places within the body as functioning members. In order to care for the members of the community, the elders have to govern the members. They do so mainly through dealing with the community as a whole. However, they should also be in a position to govern each member of the community individually as the need arises, not as a personal counselor, but as an elder and leader. The government of the individual members of the community can be expressed in instruction, admonition, encouragement or correction, but it can involve personal direction as well.

1 Thes 2:11-12, 5:14; Jn 10:3-4

1 Tm 3:1-14; Ti 1:5; Acts 6:3

Because the elders govern and lead the community as a whole, they are responsible for directing the participation of the community members in the life of the community. The elders can determine which community activities the individual members should take part in and what services they should perform for the body. The elders should consider the requests or suggestions of the members, but the final decision belongs to the elders. Moreover, when the body has a serious need, either in maintaining its life or fulfilling its mission, the leaders can call upon the right members of the community to meet that need with their time and resources, even if the call implies a significant change in the personal life of the individual or his family. The elders can expect the kind of obedience in a state of emergency similar to what a nation might expect in wartime.

The elders of the community normally do not direct the personal life of most of the members of the community. The elders only take responsibility for directing the personal lives of members of the community when there is some area that demands significant correction, or when the welfare of the body is at stake. When a decision arises that would change the shape of a person's life or affect it in a major way, the elders should be informed as soon as the decision becomes imminent. They can give their advice and that advice should be received seriously, but the elders do not normally assume responsibility for the decision.

2 Cor 8:3, 9:7; Phlm 8-9,14,21

1 Thes 5:14

The elders of the community often delegate their authority to subordinate authorities who then serve under the elders. The subordinate authorities should be received and submitted to as representatives of the elders, able to act for the community within the limits of their authority. Subordinate authorities direct the members of the community they care for in a way similar to the

Ex 18:21-27
Dt 1:14-15

elders within the sphere of responsibility the elders have entrusted to them.

### *3. Relationships with additional personal direction*

Certain relationships in the Christian community involve personal direction, often more direction than comes through the government of the elders. Members of the community belong to a family or have been accepted as members of a
Eph 5:21-6:3; family household. They therefore obey the father
Col 3:18-20 of the family, his wife as subordinate to him, or whoever replaces him because of his death or
Prv 6:20 absence. Because a family lives its daily life together and shares its resources and because the Lord has given the head of the family responsibility for the lives of the members, the members of a good family will receive a great deal of personal direction.

Many other members of the community have entered into a household in which there is a commitment together that extends to the whole of each person's life and that involves a sharing of resources. Often such households are composed of men or women who live single for the Lord. In such households the members are usually in obedience to the head of the household and normally receive a significant amount of direction for their personal lives. Any situation within the community which involves a full commitment together of life and resources will involve a full personal submission and more personal direction.

Members of the community may also enter into a relationship with the governors of the community in which they will receive much greater direction of their personal life. Sometimes they will enter into a personal training relationship for the sake of growing more rapidly and effectively into a servant of the Lord. Such relationships will normally begin with a lengthy period in which the person who is training them forms and directs their personal life. Normally as the relationship progresses the trainer gives less personal direction.

Acts 16:3; Phil 2:22; 1 Pt 5:13

Sometimes members of the community will enter into special commitments for the sake of service, usually with the elders of the community. They make their whole life available for service in the community and they are provided for by the community. Such commitments make the entire lives of these members open to the direction of those who are over them in the community. Commonly the elders of the community are themselves in such special care relationships together.

In some communities all of the members' time and resources are pooled together and directed by the elders. Such communities are usually together for a special reason, normally to perform a special Christian service or to live a special way of life, and members very often live together in a more total way. All members of such communities will normally receive a great deal of direction in their lives either from the elders or from the subordinate governors in the community.

## *4. Special purposes for personal direction*

Elders and other governors of a Christian community often give direction because they want to lead the body or the individual community member to a goal. They can give more or less direction depending on what they are trying to accomplish. All who exercise authority over others need wisdom from the Lord about the kind of direction to give and how to give it.

Direction is normally given for one of three reasons: for training (personal formation), for the care and protection of the individual, or to meet the needs or accomplish the goals of the community as a whole. When governors give direction for training their goal is to form people according to the image of Christ and to help them grow more capable in serving the Lord. Governors can give direction to anyone they are responsible for when they see that direction would help personal growth, but they normally give such direction in relationships of ongoing formation, such as the raising of children, the instruction of new Christians, and the training of community members for positions of Christian service. Direction that is given for training is usually temporary and comes to an end as the person being formed reaches maturity. Such direction aims at making the person more capable and ready to assume responsibility, not more dependent on direction from the governor in order to function. Training that involves personal direction can be a very effective means of formation and can lead people to responsibility and initiative more quickly than means which do not involve requiring them to change.

2 Tm 3:16; Ti 2:12; Prv 3:11-12, 5:12-14

When a governor attempts to care for or protect someone in need, he often has to give direction in order to be effective. Sometimes the need arises because of a personal problem. Sometimes the need is created by wrongdoing and the necessity of correction. Some members of the body are in need

1 Thes 5:14; 2 Thes 3:12

because they are not capable of directing their lives or parts of their lives on their own. Whatever the reason, members of the community often require direction in their lives either from the head of their household, an elder of the community, or some other governor in the community. No one will be totally exempt from needing such direction, and no one should become so self-reliant that he is not capable of receiving such care when it is needed.

When governors give direction in order to meet the needs and accomplish the goals of the community, their goal is to lead the individuals in the body to support the body and its mission. A father has to lead his family and so has to direct the members of the family, as do the heads of a household or service group and the elders of a community. Governors do not give such direction for the sake of the person, but to lead individuals to serve the body or other members of the body, or the mission of the body, often at the cost of sacrificing personal interests, desires and preferences. Sometimes a governor should give a great deal of such direction, sometimes very little. But no body can function effectively unless its members are receiving the kind of direction that unites them and moves them forward together. Phil 1:27-2:11

## *5. The wisdom and character of governors*

Governors need wisdom in giving direction to those they are responsible for. They should give direction firmly, fully expecting obedience and not passing over disobedience. Yet they should not be rigid and refuse to reconsider when there is good reason to do so. Governors should not

Prv 28:2, 15-16; 29:2, 4:14

assume responsibility that should be entrusted to the person they are caring for, or they will train people to be passive or timid and dependent. Yet they should lead strongly enough so that they do not encourage rebelliousness, independence or disorderliness, and so that they do not demoralize the group or lower its confidence and commitment. Governors should not demand too much or they will discourage their subordinates and make them unhappy with themselves. Yet they should not ask for too little, or they will produce a low level of commitment and service. Governors should not normally try to decide matters that are beyond their wisdom or ability, especially when those under them have more competence in the matter or acquaintance with the situation. Yet they should not abdicate responsibility for matters when they should handle them, and should seek advice, instruction or direction from someone over them when their own ability has reached its limit and they are not confident those under them will handle the situation well.

1 Tm 3:1-7; Ti 1:5-9

Those who bear the responsibility for caring for others in the Lord have a demanding task and a great need for personal Christian maturity. They should combine gentleness with firmness, grace with discipline, dignity with brotherliness, patience with zeal. They should be approachable but not overly familiar, consistent but not rigid. They must be eager to serve, dedicated to the good of

Lk 22:24-27; 1 Pt 5:2-3; Rom 12:8

those they are caring for. They should not treat people as personal favorites, but should approve those who are more dedicated and of greater maturity in Christian character. They must not be seeking a position for themselves or personal glory or gain. They should themselves be submissive and ready to obey. They should be confident in the Lord, not anxious or suspicious or excitable. They should, in short, model themselves on the good shepherd, knowing that they will have to give an account of their stewardship.

Jn 10:1-18; Mt 24:45-51, 25:14-30; Heb 13:17

## 6. *Submission*

Phil 2:12-14

The members of a Christian community should receive direction from their governors submissively. By submitting to their governors, they strengthen the body. Their submission prevents power struggles and conflicts and brings peace and unity. The greater unity frees the body to serve the Lord, and the greater peace is good soil for a deeper love among the brothers and sisters. Submission thus makes the body more effective and fruitful. At the same time, a submissive attitude allows individuals to receive much more wisdom, confidence, and protection from their governors. Submission frees the power of God to work in a body.

Phil 2:1-11; 1 Pt 5:1-5; Heb 13:17

Submission is based on a willingness to receive direction from others. In order to achieve genuine submission, Christians have to take a position of humility so that they can genuinely place themselves under others and obey them. In order to achieve true humility, they have to put aside their rebelliousness, their independence, their self-importance, their desire for power, their desire to have their own way, their attachment to their personal preferences and pleasures, and their self-concern and self-protectiveness. They must put aside, in short, all self-will and all that leads to willfulness. Submission demands a freedom from self that is part of the character of Jesus.

Submission involves obedience, but it involves more than looking for commands and obeying them. Often the governor entrusts responsibility for an area or a decision to the subordinate, and Mt 25:14-23 submission then means being faithful to the responsibility. Often the governor gives advice and leaves the decision to the subordinate. Submission in such cases does not mean pressing for a decision from the governor, but rather accepting the governor's commission. Nor does submission mean being passive. People can be active in submission—taking responsibility for their life and the things entrusted to them, showing initiative, discussing the directions they receive from their governor—especially when their efforts stem from a desire to cooperate with their governor.

Submission likewise involves relating well to a governing authority in whose judgment or abilities one does not have the fullest confidence. It means helping and not opposing, offering advice or even respectful correction rather than challenge. It means normally giving the governing authority the benefit of the doubt. It means seeking advice from the next higher governing authority about how to relate well to the governor causing one the difficulty and about how to handle situations where something important is at issue. It means, in short, subordinating oneself and one's views about what would be best to the strength of the cooperative effort, not always simply acquiescing in the direction given, but always dealing with situations in a cooperative spirit and in a way that strengthens the body.

Eph 5:22, 6:5 Submitting to human beings can be a way of submitting to the Lord. When Christians submit to those who are over them in the Lord or who have authority from the Lord, then their submission is obedience to the Lord. When they feel that they are receiving directions from the Lord (leadings of the Spirit or other revelations), they can follow them if they are confident in them, but they should submit these directions to their governors for discernment if the matter is significant. Submission to a human being is not a substitute for a relationship with God. Rather, submission to human beings is something God works through to form his people in his own likeness, to train them in submission to himself, and to protect them from self-delusion and the deception of evil spirits. 1 Jn 4:20

Submission to Christian authority can only be based on the fear of the Lord. Members of a Christian community submit their lives to the elders of the body as to men who have been given position and authority by the Lord and who therefore are to be respected out of fear of the Lord. Members of the community approach the elders as men who represent a body that the Lord has called together, and who therefore speak for the body and command the same commitment and honor as the body itself. The members of the community should respect the elders not simply as brothers in the Lord but as men upon whom the Lord has conferred authority, and their submission to the elders should come from this respect. Eph 5:21; Nm 12:1-16, 16:1-50

## 7. *Appeal*

When subordinates experience difficulty in accepting their governor's directions, the differences normally can be resolved through discussion. Sometimes, however, a subordinate is faced with a direction that his governor will not change and the subordinate does not want to accept. Most commonly these difficulties arise because the subordinate prefers a different approach or feels that a different approach would work better. Such difficulties are an opportunity to put aside preferences and opinions and grow in submission. But sometimes a difficulty arises because the subordinate, using Christian judgment, cannot accept the governor's decision as being right. Out of concern for the Lord and the body, the subordinate should continue to seek a resolution to the difficulty in a respectful and submissive way.

Sometimes difficulties arise when subordinates judge that the governor's directions are a serious mistake, leading to results that would be harmful. Subordinates can then appeal the decision. They should first ask the governor who made the decision to reconsider. Then, if they are not satisfied with the results, they can appeal to the next higher governor. In so doing they should let the governor from whom they are appealing know about the appeal. They can keep appealing to higher governors until the appeal is no longer received. If the judgment finally goes against them, they should accept it, submitting their judgment to their governors. If for some reason they find it impossible to accept the judgment as correct, they should obey it and entrust the matter to the Lord, the lord over all governors.

Occasionally the difficulty arises because the subordinates judge that the governor's direction would lead to some sort of unrighteousness, either breaking one of the Lord's commandments or unfaithfulness to a serious commitment. If either were the case, to obey would be unrighteous and the subordinates could not obey. Before reaching such a conclusion, subordinates should investigate their own judgment. Their judgment could be wrong and their governor's right, and they have to answer for a rash judgment. Normally they should discuss the matter with the governor who gave the direction and with higher governors. If, at the end of the process, the subordinates are convinced that the issue is one of unrighteousness, then their responsibility is to refuse to accept the direction given them.

Community members who are having a difficulty with directions that have been given them by their governors should conduct themselves in a loyal way. They can sometimes ask advice from a mature member of the community, but they should not speak about the difficulty to very many. They should not bring the matter to someone outside the community except to those who might have authority over the elders of the community in the matter at issue. They should not speak about the difficulty to anyone else outside of the community, for to do so would be disloyal and would bring reproach on the Lord's work. In everything, they should conduct themselves in such a way as to maintain the unity of the body and its good name and should trust the Lord to care adequately for the difficulty. Rom 8:28

## *8. Authority and love*

Direction and submission in Christian community should always function within a loving relationship. Those who give direction and those who submit to it are committed to one another in brotherly love as members of Christ. Those who exercise authority have the responsibility to care

1 Thes 5:13, 2:7-8; Eph 4:1-6, 4:31-32

for those they have authority over. Those who submit to authority have the responsibility to cooperate with their governors and receive their directions willingly. Each should desire to make the relationship a joy to the other. Governing authorities should have a reverence for the responsibility that has been entrusted to them. Subordinates should be grateful for being served by their governors. Both should love one another out of love for Christ.

## Notes

a. This section depends for its relationship to the previous one on the distinction between correction and direction (see Glossary). The previous section was concerned with matters of correction and discipline. This section is concerned mainly with direction of people's personal lives when an objective standard of righteousness is not the basis of the direction. A governmental relationship involves both authoritative direction and correction. The approach in this section is also based on the distinction between participation in the things a body does together and what a person does on his own. It is clear to many that the community's elders have authority over the things a body does together. This section states that the elders also have authority over the individual's life in all aspects, because community means having everything in common, but that they do not have the right to direct everything in a person's life except under certain circumstances. Rather than base the description of direction in the community on a legal definition of rights and duties, this section proceeds from a distinction between what is normally done and what can be done under special circumstances.

# VI. Unity and Disagreement

## 1. Unity

The Lord desires each body of Christians to be one, even as he and the Father are one. He offers Jn 17:20-23 Christians a oneness which manifests his glory and the Father's love to the world. Without that unity Christians cannot witness to the world with full power. With that unity, they can already realize Acts 4:32-33; Phil 1:27-28 the power and victory of the Lord in their midst. Phil 1:28

The bond of peace, that is, of good, loving Eph 4:3 relationships, preserves the unity of the Spirit. When there is mutual love in a body of Christians, that body can be one. Service, obedience, self-sacrifice, and care build unity in a body of Christians. Unity involves more than an absence of division and conflict. Christian unity means loving one another as the Father loves the Son and the Son loves the Father. As Christians learn how to love one another with the love of the Father and Son, they will forge bonds among them that will resist all the attacks of the enemy.

A loving unity depends upon government and 1 Cor 11:3; Phil 2:1-16 submission. As the Son obeys the Father and subordinates his life to the Father's authority, and as the members of the human body order themselves under the head, so also a body of Christians needs government and submission to preserve the order which allows love and unity to grow and to be effective. The elders and other governing authorities in the Christian community are responsible to teach and direct the body, to lead it forward in unity. Only when the rest of the body submits to them and receives their direction can full unity be established.

Acts 4:32; Phil 1:27, 2:2

The Lord wants a oneness for his people that is more than external. He wants a oneness of mind and heart that is founded on assent to his revealed truth, the following of the leading of his Spirit, and the wisdom he gives about how to live and serve together in the circumstances he sets us in. Such a oneness depends on elders who lead the community well. It depends on them having the character, training, gifts and abilities to lead effectively. It depends on them following the Lord faithfully, studying his teaching, seeking for his direction, and doing his will eagerly as they discover it. It depends on them coming to a oneness of mind or a common decision about how to handle situations, handling disagreements among themselves well and not spreading them to members of the community.[a.] Finally, it depends on the elders leading the community wisely and justly into accepting the teaching of the Lord or the common direction.

The oneness of the Lord likewise depends on the response of the community members who should seek oneness with those who govern them and who should seek to have a body that can live and act in unity. They need the humility of mind that allows them to acknowledge others as over them in the Lord and that allows them to be

Phil 2:3

taught, directed and corrected. While such a

humility does not involve automatically giving up one's own understanding, it does involve willingness to give those in authority the benefit of the doubt, to be as cooperative as possible when the elders give direction and to handle all disagreements or disputes in a way that preserves the unity of the body. To live out the unity the Lord wants requires effort from his people. The model he sets Eph 5:3
before them is the oneness between the Father and the Son, a oneness of mind and heart, not a oneness achieved by an effective human arrangement, or a clever human compromise, or the force of external authority.

All community members, including the elders, must submit to the Lord's ideal of unity for his people in order to be an effective member of a body. Many in the world hold up the ideal of independence of judgment and diversity of viewpoint, but in so doing they betray the fact that they are committed to individualism and not to genuine community. For Christians, the higher value is the love of God and of their brothers and sisters that involves a unity of mind and heart. They therefore place a lower value on developing an individuality of approach or a more correct opinion than they do on coming to a oneness of understanding with the Christian community they are part of and on living the same truth together with their brothers and sisters.

## *2. Conflict and meekness*

Members of a Christian community could choose to approach discussion and disagreement in a spirit of conflict or in a spirit of meekness. When a spirit of conflict prevails, disunity results and love

Rom 8:6; 1 Cor 3:3

ebbs away. When a spirit of meekness prevails, unity grows and love thrives. Christians cannot approach disagreement in a spirit that comes from the world, the flesh, and Satan, and still expect to be a body of people who love one another.

Gal 5:19-21, 26; Eph 4:31; 2 Cor 12:20; Ti 3:10

Those who approach discussion and disagreement in a spirit of conflict attempt to influence direction by applying pressure. Sometimes their attempts openly manifest conflict and hostility, and their speech and actions are characterized by attacks, abuse, and even physical violence. Sometimes their attempts manifest conflict and hostility in a more indirect way. Their words are characterized by argumentativeness, criticism, or a desire to debate. They often place a high value on protest, confrontation, moral intimidation and public criticism or attack. They sometimes organize with others into factions and begin campaigns in order to gain greater power in influencing the directions in which a body might move. All these approaches, whether direct or indirect, grow out of conflict and hostility. Sometimes the conflict and hostility simply come out of the willfulness that is rooted in the flesh. Sometimes they come from a conviction that conflict is the best way to raise issues and get action. Underlying such a conviction is the view that force, at least in the form of resistance, whether physical or verbal, is needed to see that the affairs of the body are directed in the right way.

Those who approach questions about the direcation of the body in a spirit of conflict often believe that everyone has the same responsibility for the direction of the body, and that the body as a whole is the proper forum for discussion. They feel entitled to advocate whatever they judge to be proper, and to make their opinions heard whenever it seems good to them. While they may recognize the need to entrust final decision-making to another body, they will not accept a limitation on discussion or enter into any submission to the judgment of the body responsible for direction.

Phil 2:1-12; Gal 5:22-23

The spirit that prevails in a Christian community should be a spirit of meekness, the spirit of those who know that they are servants of the Lord and of one another. A Christian community should be free of conflict, hostility, protest, factions and party-spirit. Christians should enter discussion in good faith, trusting that their brothers and sisters will give their words a good hearing and will want to know the truth and follow it. They should also have a trust that the Lord will lead his people. Therefore, they can rely on directly and peacefully speaking the truth rather than on using pressure or conflict to further their own views.

1 Tm 4:11; 2 Tm 4:2-5; Ti 1:13, 2:1, 15,3:8; 2 Cor 10:1-6

In a Christian community, concern for the direction of the community should also be based upon an acceptance of the authority of the elders in the community for decision-making. Thus, the spirit of meekness also manifests itself in a cooperative and submissive spirit. Christians should be willing to receive and to accept a decision that differs from their own. The spirit of meekness and cooperativeness, however, should not lead to reticence and unwillingness to be open in discussion. Peacefulness and brotherly love should lead to a greater mutual trust and a greater ability to speak freely. Christians should be able to give their opinions directly and firmly to those responsible for the matters that they are concerned about. Those in authority should be all the more ready to listen because they know that the Lord can speak through any member of the body.

## *3. Handling discussions of approach*

A Christian community will experience discussion and disagreement in questions of approach, of major directions, and of teaching (fundamental principles and truths). Each area should be handled somewhat differently.

Members of a Christian community should take an active concern for the approaches taken in community life and service (for instance, the manner in which singing is used in worship, or the way in which events are scheduled). When they see something that they think could be improved, they should share their opinion. They should,
Eph 4:29; Phil 2:14 however, speak in a constructive way. When their evaluation is negative, they should only speak to someone responsible for the area about which they are concerned, and should not complain about how the area is being handled to people who have no responsibility for it. When they feel that their concern is a serious one, they should ask that their suggestion be seriously weighed, and if they do not receive an affirmative response, they may speak to the person who is next highest in responsibility if they are convinced that the matter is important enough. They should, however, accept that the final decision belongs to those who are responsible.

Those who hold responsibility for the life and service of the community should be eager to receive input from others in the community about their area of responsibility. They should take suggestions and negative evaluation seriously: a comment that is given them might well be coming from the Lord. When a suggestion is serious and they do not agree with it, they should normally give an account of their own approach to the interested person. They should be committed to taking seriously the concerns of their brothers and sisters.

## *4. Handling discussions of major direction*

Everyone in the community can have a role in the direction of the community. Each person can give an opinion of his own or some word from the Lord, and his comment might direct the community in a significant way. Moreover, in a community that comes before the Lord in worship in a way that allows the Lord to speak, much of the direction will be given as the community responds together to the Lord. Yet the body of elders or the presiding elder, subject to the governing authority that may be over the community, has the responsibility for major decisions in the community. While they should listen to the contributions of the members of the community and can consult them formally and informally, the proper governing authority can make decisions for the community and expect the community to accept those decisions and to support them.

1 Cor 14:26

When a member of the community seriously disagrees with a major directional decision the proper governing authorities have made, he can ask for a reconsideration. He can also request a consultation of a wider group within the community before the decision becomes final, or request that he be allowed to make an appeal to any authorities that may be over the community. He should, however, be subject to the directions of the proper governing authority in how he pursues the matter further.

Governing authorities may allow discussion in the body after they have made a decision. If a decision provokes widespread dissatisfaction, they would be wise to study the matter further until they are able to understand the reasons for the dissatisfaction and respond to them well. Governing authorities should be ready to change their decision if they discover good reasons to do so. They should also be willing to close discussion of the issue in the community if further discussion would be harmful, and the members of the community should submit to their decision.

A community should be able to seek the Lord together about directional matters. A community should also be able to receive directions from its leaders and submit to them. Its ability to serve the Lord will often depend on its ability to either discuss or obey as is appropriate. The body of elders or the presiding elder has the authority to determine which approach is the wise one, and the unity and effectiveness of the community depends upon the members' ability to accept the judgment of the proper authority.

## *5. Handling discussion of teaching*

The body of elders or the presiding elder is responsible for supervising the teaching in the community and for deciding which principles the community will follow in a given area. Much community teaching may be given by members with responsibilities for teaching in areas of community life, or may come through the sharing of insight or inspiration by any member of the community, but the final responsibility for overseeing all community teaching belongs to the proper governing authority, subject to any governing authorities that may be over the community.

1 Cor 12:28, 14:26
Col 3:16

When a member of the community seriously disagrees with something in community teaching, he can ask the proper governing authority to reconsider it or appeal if such appeal is possible. If all appeal is exhausted, he should accept the decision. Normally he should submit his judgment to the governing authorities as to men over him in the Lord. Sometimes he will be unable to do so, and then he should inform the elders of his reasons but not oppose the community teaching to others. If the disagreement does not involve denial of basic Christian doctrine, normally the elders will allow the person to remain a part of the community and will help him to approach the area in a constructive way.

## 6. *Discussion in love*

God is love, and love is essential to a Christian community. Many in modern society put the highest value on opinions, policies and approaches. But in a Christian community the highest value is placed upon a loving relationship to God and to the brothers and sisters. To love God we must be faithful to his truth, and our love for one another must be based on our faithfulness to God. Nonetheless, more effort should go into building one another up and serving the Lord than

1 Jn 4:7-12; 1 Pt 4:8;
Eph 4:15-16

into discussing issues, debating policies and evaluating performance. When love is valued rightly, many of the causes of disunity disappear.

Eph 4:25, 29; 5:19-20 Almost anything within the Christian community can be discussed if the discussion is carried on in a way that builds up the body. In fact, a Christian community should be the place in which the freest discussion can be carried on, because the members of the community can count upon one another's commitment to the body and to Christian love. In determining whether a discussion should be carried on or approached differently, the most helpful criterion is that of whether or not the body is being built up and strengthened.

Col 4:5-6 Christian love involves loyalty, and loyalty to the community involves keeping community disagreements within the community, except when those disagreements can and should be brought to people with governing authority over the community. It is disloyalty to go to people outside the community in order to put pressure on the community to change. It is disloyalty to expose community difficulties to the media or to people at large outside the community. It is disloyalty to draw others into disagreements within the community in any way. Loyalty involves relating to people outside in a way that will increase their respect for the community and for the Lord.

Ti 3:1-7 Most Christian communities exist in a society that does not approach unity in the same way that the Lord teaches about it. Often, the approach for relating to our brothers and sisters in the Lord cannot be fully followed outside the community. Members of a community should expect such differences and should have the wisdom to know how to deal with them. There are, after all, few bodies which are seriously committed to being one as the Father and Son are one. Yet that is the glory that the Lord Jesus wants to give to his body.

## *Notes*

a. The statement does not cover questions of disagreement within a body of elders. Every body of elders needs to have procedures for decision-making; procedures for handling situations when a decision cannot be reached; and procedures for handling a matter when one or more of the elders believes that good order or procedure has been violated or when he cannot accept an important directional or teaching decision. Most commonly, there should be recourse outside the body of elders. The spirit and approach presented in this section, however, will be fundamental for resolving disagreements among the elders as well.

# VII. Patterns of Life[a.]

## 1. Life together

Acts 2:40-47; Heb 10:23-25; Dt 16:1-17

The members of a Christian community hold their lives in common. Their commitment—to love and serve the Lord as one body—reaches to everything in their lives. The life of the community, therefore, extends beyond the activities and services that support the common life, reaching to what the brothers and sisters do throughout the day: at home, at work, in informal contacts. Yet at the same time, no community could function as a body without certain activities and services which form the life of the body and make outreach successful. The patterns of life in a community should be faithfully supported by the members of the community.

## 2. Smaller units

Ex 18:21-27; Dt 1:14-15 Rom 15:5; 1 Cor 16:19; Col 4:15; Phlm 2

A Christian community includes smaller groupings within the larger body. Within the smallest units, brothers and sisters who know one another and are in regular contact can build each other up in the Lord. All members of the community should have a group of brothers and sisters for whom they have personal care and who care for them in turn.

Eph 4:16; Col 2:19

The smallest groupings should be tied into larger groupings as needed so that each unit is an organic part of the larger body, of serving and being served. The larger groupings can support many of the vital functions of the community. The elders watch over all the groupings within the community, seeing that all of the subunits are linked with the body in such a way that each member of the community knows that he belongs to the entire body as fully as he does to any smaller grouping, and that each grouping cares for the welfare of the rest of the body as it does for its own.

A Christian community is also built upon natural relationships restored in Christ. God created the human race male and female in order that they might marry, have children, and form families. The parents raise their children. Relatives provide help for those closely related to them. In all these relationships God has established a natural order—with the husband being the head of the wife, the parents being in authority over the children, the older family members and relatives deserving the respect and honor of the younger. Within the wider community, patterns of respect and honor according to age and sex preserve a Christian reverence for the dignity and role of each person. Family loyalty, kinship loyalty, and natural honor and respect should strengthen and deepen the love which brothers and sisters in one body have for one another, and should not become substitutes for a wider love for the whole body. Natural groupings should strengthen and serve the body as a whole.

Gen 1-2; Mt 19:3-6; 1 Cor 11:2-3

Eph 5:22-6:4; 1 Pt 3: 1-7; Col 3:18-21; Heb 13:4

1 Tm 5:1-2,3-8; Lv 19:32; 1 Kgs 2:19

The larger community should strengthen and support the families' community life and the relationships in it provide an environment in which family relations can thrive and be supplemented. The elders in the community should back up the authority of the father as the head of the family, and the parents as governors and trainers of the child, while at the same time providing the teaching, the formation and the safeguards which make the government of the family more effective and more in accordance with Christian teaching. The stronger the family life is, the stronger the community is.

### *3. Gatherings*

The life of each Christian community centers upon the Lord himself, and each community must therefore gather before the Lord in such a way that it truly worships him as God and Lord, and in order that he can speak to them and build them up. While there can be many types of community gatherings, there should be some regular gatherings at which the community assembles as a body before the Lord. Such gatherings should be open to the participation of the community and should be ordered by the elders so that the body can come together in oneness and power.

Heb 10:25; Ex 19:17 Dt 31:28-30; Jos 24:1; 2 Chr 20:4-5, 13; Ps(s) 99/100, 121/122

### *4. Services*

A Christian community entrusts to many of its members special service responsibilities within the body or as a part of the body's outreach. Many services are best organized into jobs or projects, giving rise to special groupings and activities within the community. Some of these services build up the basic units of the community or care for individual members of the community. Some of these services are support services, providing the body with administrative or other help. Some of the services take on special areas of concern

1 Cor 12:28

such as music or evangelism. All jobs and service groupings should strengthen the basic groupings of the community, and should not supplant them in such a way that the community becomes a service organization. Nor should special service jobs and projects become so important that they displace the basic service of all the community members that takes place in daily living and in unorganized ways. The elders order the service jobs and projects in the body so as to make them a source of strength to the service of the body as a whole.

## *5. Individual contributions*

Community members perform their most important service within the context of their major commitments in life, especially family and occupation. In these situations they build up the body and bring the good news of salvation to others. In these situations they care for others and reveal the life of the Lord. Yet all the members of the community are responsible for the needs of the community in its life and mission together, and they should contribute to it generously from their resources. Members will set aside time both for participation in community activities and for whatever services they are called upon to perform. Members will also make available their financial and material resources for the needs of the body.

Neh 3-4; Acts 8:4; 1 Pt 4:8-11; 1 Tm 5:10
Ex 35:4-29; 1 Chr 29: 1-20; Nm 18:21-32; Mal 3:6-12; Acts 2:45, 4:34-35; Rom 12:13; 2 Cor 9:6-15

The extent to which members can contribute of their time and material resources to the body in its life and mission together will vary from person to person. Some will make the larger part of their time and resources available to community activities and services, while others will be able to make less of these things available, due to the demands of family and secular occupation.

The elders are responsible for watching over the contributions made by members of the community to the needs of the body and of their brothers and sisters, taking a concern for all the obligations in each person's life. They can call upon the members of the body to make personal sacrifices that enable the body to fulfill the Lord's call or that allow all the needs of the members of the body to be met. They should, at the same time, encourage and protect each individual's service of the Lord in his or her daily life outside of community activities and services, so that the life of the Lord can reach to everyone in the land.

## 6. *Receiving new brothers and sisters*

A Christian community is a body of people who live the life of Christ. No one can truly contribute to its life without being alive in Christ. Nor can those who are under bondage of sin, self or Satan be much more than a difficulty to the body. No one, therefore, should be received as a member who is not alive in Christ and free to live as a Christian.

Jn 3:3-5; 1 Jn 3:7-10

Those who are being brought into the body must leave the world and the life of sin and enter into life in Christ. Before they can be fully received as part of the body and fully responsible members of it, they must have come to genuine faith in Christ and in his work in their life. They must have turned away from all unrighteousness and turned to obedience in Christ. They must

Col 1:13; Ti 2:11-14, 3:3-7; Heb 6:1-2

Jn 1:12, 3:16; Rom 10:9; Gal 2:20 Mk 1:15; Acts 2:38, 3:19; Rom 6:16-19;

have been delivered from all serious bondage to evil spirits. They must have been baptized in water, dying and rising in Christ, and have been sealed in the Holy Spirit, coming to a genuine experience of his presence and power and gifts in their life. They must have been taught a basic understanding of Christian truth and Christian life and been led to an ongoing life of prayer and communion with God, to a righteousness of life, and to a maturity of Christian character. They must have been brought into a living relationship with the community, showing a genuine love and service towards their brothers and sisters, a proven submission to those over them in the community, and an unfeigned loyalty to the body.

Mt 12:22-29, 10:1; Acts 5:16; Eph 6:11-12

Mt 28:19; Jn 3:5-8; Rom 6: 3-4; Eph 1:13-14; Col 2: 12; Gal 3:1-4; 1 Jn 3:24; Heb 6:1-2; 1 Jn 2:22-23; Rom 6:17; Gal 6:6; 1 Tm 5:17; Ti 2:1 1 Jn 1:6-7, 2:6, 3:8,24

1 Jn 2:9-11, 3:14-17, 4:12

When new people come to the community they can be received as Christians upon their own profession,[b] but they should not be received as fully responsible members of the body unless they have been fully responsible members of a similar community and come with that community's recommendation. Without such recommendation they should go through a period of preparation until the elders are assured that their faith and their life are sound. Likewise, children of community members should go through a period of preparation before being admitted to fully responsible membership. For both groups their preparation time should normally last until they demonstrate ongoing faithfulness to the life of the community, a good spirit in their commitment to the community and its leaders, and a stability and consistency in their Christian living. This stability involves an ability to relate in a loving way with others, especially those they live with and are close to, an ability to be faithful to responsibilities, and a regular prayer life. The elders should know them well enough to be assured that they are free of bondage to evil spirits and are sound in Christian belief. The elders should not receive people as fully responsible members too readily, but only upon the evidence of full spiritual life and genuine love.

## 7. *Valuing patterns of life*

The structures and patterns of life in a body do not constitute the life of the body. A corpse has much the same form after it has died as it had when it was alive. A body of Christians must be primarily concerned with its spiritual life, its faith, its obedience, its worship of the Lord, the commitment and love of its members for one another and for the whole body, and the eagerness of its members to serve all men and to bring to them the life of Christ. Yet no body can grow soundly without a pattern of life that is appropriate to its nature as a Christian community. The Lord gives wisdom to his people, enabling them to order their ways so as to follow him. All the members of the body must be dedicated to care for and to protect those elements of their life together that make it possible for them to be one body, serving the Lord.

# Notes

a. The statement does not explicitly treat questions of approaches to worship and questions of church ordinances or sacraments.

b. The statement allows for different approaches to receiving those who profess Christianity. It requires, however, that elders have a reasonable assurance of their soundness of faith and life before admitting them to fully responsible membership, regardless of the approach taken to their standing as Christians.

# *Glossary*

**Common life** and **life together**: The statement makes a distinction between the common life of a community and the things the members of the community do together. The life together of the community refers to those activities and services which community members do together with other members of the community as community members. It refers to things done by the whole community together (e.g. gatherings of the whole community, maintainance of a common fund), as well as things done by subgroupings (e.g. a gathering of a part of the community, a meeting of a community evangelistic outreach). The common life of the community includes everything the members of the community do in life, because their commitment together reaches to everything, even when they are not together with other members of the community. Outside of community activities and services, community members can carry on the community's work of evangelism, make money to support the community mission, and build up a brother or sister in the Lord. Many of the most significant events in the life of a Christian community occur outside of community activities and services.

**Correction**: "Correction" is used in the broad sense of setting right what is wrong according to a standard of righteousness.It includes all types of activity which can be corrective: teaching, admonition, encouragement, and exhortation, as well as reproof, rebuke, and punishment, which are means of correction in the narrower sense.

**Direct responsibility**: When someone has a direct responsibility, he can be held accountable if he does not take action and do what he can to correct the situation. When direct responsibility for a situation belongs to others, a person can act if he sees a way to make a helpful contribution, but he is not bound to do so.

**Discipline**: "Discipline" is used as an equivalent to the scriptural terms *musar-paideia*. It means the process of training, but a process of training which is backed up by authority and enforcement. Hence it commonly means correction of wrongdoing and punishment.

**Government** and **direction**: "Government" is used as the broad term to describe all that a governing authority does. It includes correction, discipline, teaching, and encouragement, as well as direction. Most government is teaching the way of Jesus and encouraging, correcting, or training people to follow it. "Direction" here is reserved for any command which is not simply commanding an objective standard of righteousness but involves directing someone in a concrete situation beyond what is covered by law or teaching.

**Governmental authorities - governors - those responsible for someone - those over someone**: These phrases are used equivalently. They refer primarily to the elders, but they also refer to any Christian authority that has responsibility for others, including subheads under the elders and parents of families.